GLORIOUS TREASURES
The Celts

First published in Great Britain in 1997 by
Brockhampton Press,
20 Bloomsbury Street,
London WC1B 3QA
A member of the Hodder Headline Group

ISBN 1 86019 563 6

A copy of the CIP data is available upon request from the
British Library.

Produced for Brockhampton Press by Flame Tree Publishing,
a part of The Foundry Creative Media Company Ltd,
The Long House, Antrobus Road, Chiswick, London W4 5HY

GLORIOUS TREASURES
The Celts

Karen Sullivan
with Penny Clarke

BROCKHAMPTON PRESS

Contents

Introduction

f all the ancient peoples of Europe, the Celts are probably the most intriguing, not least because they have never, at any point in their history, had a national identity. Indeed, the term 'Celts' embraces peoples who are as geographically disparate as they are varied in their traditions. The Celts were an ancient European people who probably came from the distant steppes of Central Asia beyond the Caspian Sea. By 500 BC they inhabited north-eastern France, south-western Germany and Bohemia, from where they continued to migrate in all directions. Around 400 BC Celtic tribes crossed the Swiss Alps into northern Italy. After capturing the fertile Po Valley region, they laid siege to Rome. At the same time other groups of Celts pushed down into France and Spain, eastward to Asia Minor, and westward to the British Isles. In Asia Minor they founded the kingdom of Galatia (St Paul's Epistle to the Galatians in the New Testament is addressed to the descendants of these Celts). In Britain, Celtic warriors overran and conquered the islands, and it is here that their influence is most apparent today.

Over a period that spanned nearly two and a half thousand years – from about 1650 BC to AD 900, the Celtic culture survived with a unique style and unsurpassed quality of craftsmanship and artistic vision. The Celts have always been surrounded by an aura of romance and intrigue. They have been described as a race of ancient mystics – an image fed by their lyrical, mysterious literature and their gruesome pagan religious observances – and the genius of their artistic craftsmanship has inspired wonder for centuries. Yet, they have also been reviled for their savageness and ferocity – an exquisite artistic integrity superimposed on a barbarian psyche. The Celts who inhabited England, Wales, Ireland and parts of Scotland in the five hundred years before the birth of Christ left no written history, but their treasures reveal a profoundly artistic and enlightened culture, with jewellery, weapons, armour, metal fittings, manuscripts and sculpture beautifully decorated with fascinating and powerful designs. The art of the Celts is their legacy, and it tells their tale.

The Cross of Cong was created in AD 1123 for the King of Connacht. It is made from oak encased in copper and silver sheets with beautiful and intricate engraving.

Model Rain Chariot

Black is the season of deep winter,
The margins of the world are storm-crested,
Sad are the birds of every meadow,
Lamenting the harsh winter's clamour
All save ravens gorged on blood.
Winter – rough-black, dark-smoked, cold-flinted,
Dogs splinter the cracking bones,
Cauldrons sit on fires at the dark day's end.
Celtic blessing of winter

Early Iron Age art, of which this piece forms a part, is (particularly in Britain) usually abstract, with the merest hints of faces, animal forms, and shape-changing beasts. However, there are some less ambiguous representations in Celtic art, especially in Ireland, where bird motifs and sculpture are highly stylized. The Hallstatt Celts, who originated in what is now Austria, are noted for their development of motifs, notably of birds (especially waterfowl) which appear on a wide variety of objects. The duck on this chariot may represent an association with a water cult, and it has been suggested that the wheels are the Hallstatt version of the sun discs of earlier times. It is not known what a rain chariot would have been used for, except perhaps for some cultic purpose, for birds were sacred in Celtic mythology.

This Celtic rain chariot with the figure of a duck was possibly used for cultic purposes.
It dates from the mid-1st millennium BC.

Bronze Animals

'I'll come before you in the shape of a harmless red heifer and
lead the cattle-herd to trample you in the waters, by ford and
pond, and you will not know me.'
'Then I'll hurl a stone at you,' he said, 'and break your leg and
you will carry that mark until the end of your days unless I lift
it from you with a blessing.'
Unknown Celtic Author, *The Cattle Raid of Cooley (Tain Bo Cuailgne)*

Animal figurines were often buried in Celtic graves as substitutes for the animals themselves. Bronze figurines depicting cows, for instance, would be found in graves belonging to people from a herding society. A model horse might be placed in the grave of someone who was not rich enough to have a horse killed and buried, together with its accoutrements, in the tomb with him. Bulls, boars, sheep and dogs played an important role in Celtic iconography, for instance boars represent ferocity and cunning, and are mentioned many times in Celtic mythology: a white boar leads Pryderi into slavery in Annwn, and another boar is the cause of Diarmuid's death. Boar imagery occurs everywhere in Celtic lands – as figurines, crests, stamps on swords and on coins – and it is usually believed to represent warfare and supreme power. Dogs are depicted to represent the faithful servant of humanity, and in Celtic mythology are usually one of the animals that aid the hero in his quest.

A selection of small bronze animal figures, including a Celtic bronze rabbit
dating from c. 1st–2nd centuries AD.

Bronze Statuettes

Brighid of the Mantle, encompass us,
Lady of the Lambs, protect us,
Keeper of the Hearth, kindle us.
Beneath your mantle, gather us,
And restore us to memory.
Celtic blessing

During their occupation of Britain, the Romans gave many of the nature gods names similar to those of their own deities. However, some gods were not given Roman names, either because the locals were incensed that their gods or goddesses should have anything other than a Celtic name, or because the Romans were overwhelmed by the god's wide range of attributes – too diverse, perhaps, to fit neatly the characteristics of an individual Roman deity.

This bronze of a male is typically stern and appears to carry a sword. It is probably cast bronze, heavily beaten and rather crudely made. The bronze of the female represents Athena.

Romano-Celtic bronze statuettes of standing deities, measuring approximately
8.4 cm in height. These date from c. 1st century AD.

Sheet Bronze Figure with Torque

I liked to walk in the river meadows
In the thick of the dew and the morning shadows,
At the edge of the woods in a deep defile
At peace with myself in the first sunshine.
When I looked at Lough Graney, my heart grew bright,
Ploughed lands, and green, in the morning light,
Mountains in rows with crimson borders …
Unknown Celtic Author, 'The Midnight Court' (Cuirt an Mhean-Oiche)

It appears that the Celts had no interest in either narrative art or pictorial realism. This is assumed because their artwork contains very few representations of the people themselves or of their way of life. Their images of men are limited to some enormous stone statues, a few bronze busts, small doll-like men and a multitude of heads. Very few full-length human figures are known to exist, and there are almost no representations of females.

This figure is worked in sheet bronze, and the more naturalistic representation indicates a Roman influence. Why the Celts preferred the abstract, and the reason for the absence of human figures in their art is not known. One theory is that it may be due to a religious taboo on the representation of the human form or on narrative sequences, as is the case with Jewish and Muslim art.

This figure, cast from sheet bronze, is wearing a torque. It dates from the last days of Celtic sovereignty before the Romans seized power.

Tanderagee Stone Figure

Here on Dairbhreach's lonely wave
For years to come your watery home
No Lir nor druid can now ye save
From endless wandering on the lonely foam.
Unknown Celtic Author, 'The Children of Lir'

This stone figure is dated between 250 BC and AD 250, and is believed to have come from a powerful pagan sanctuary at Armagh Hill, Ireland. It is made of sandstone and has vestigial horns, moustaches, a great mouth and a wild appearance. It has been described as wearing a horned helmet, but this is now believed to be an illusion created by the long, straight eyebrow line, which terminates at the side of the head. Many Celtic stone sculptures have humanized arms stretched across the body, and some archeologists believe that such an attitude has spiritual significance.

The figure may have been displayed on a burial mound, or perhaps housed in a shrine which the Christian establishment suppressed in later times. This particular example of Irish stone sculpture closely parallels the pagan iconography found in areas of Celtic Europe. Stone remained one of the main mediums for the Celtic sculptors until the Iron Age, after which it seems to have been seldom used.

This Tanderagee stone figure may have come from a pagan shrine
discovered on the hill of Armagh, Ireland.

Carved Wooden Figure

They wear ornaments of gold, torques on their necks, and
bracelets on their arms and wrists, while people of high rank
wear dyed garments besprinkled with gold.
Strabo, Historian *c.* 63 BC – AD 24

A carved wooden figure found at Ralaghan, Co. Cavan. This is a very important find for two reasons: first, wood decays easily, particularly in damp climates, so very little Celtic woodwork survives; second, full-length figures are extremely rare in Celtic art.

The stylized nature of this figure makes it difficult to determine with any certainty whether it represents a man or a woman. However, the hole suggests that it is likely to have been a male figure with a detachable penis (long since lost) that would have fitted into the hole. Support for this theory comes from the fact that the Celts were a nomadic people who originated in central Europe. There they came into contact with the Greeks and Romans, and several small male figures with removable penises have been found in association with Roman remains.

Both the Greeks and Romans have left written accounts of the Celts. Indeed, the word *Celt* derives from the Greek *Keltoi*. It is first known to have been used in the sixth century BC, when the Greeks referred to a group of warriors with a distinctive language as being *Keltoi*. To the Greeks it was a perjorative term, but as they tended to view anyone and anything non-Greek as inferior, much of the known world at that time came into that category.

This carved wooden figure is probably a male, as it is possible that a detachable penis would once have been fitted into the hole.

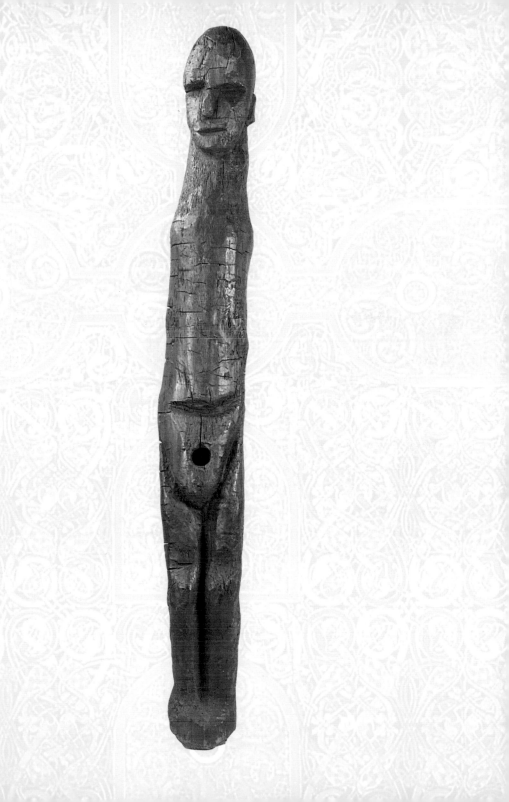

Harness Mount

And green and golden I was
huntsman and herdsman, the calves
Sang to my horn, the foxes on the hills
barked clear and cold.
Dylan Thomas

This coloured harness mount dates from around the first century BC, and its decoration is indicative of the lavish technique used for equine accoutrements of the time. For the Celts, horses were figures of reverence. As well as being the illustrious mounts of goddesses, they are mentioned throughout Celtic folklore, most prominently as mythical beings taking the shape of a horse. There is evidence of a school of metalwork which produced nothing but richly decorated enamelled harness mounts. The enamelling on this piece – coral and yellow – is Mediterranean in style, and the enamel was likely to have been imported from there. The lines made by the compass to pick out the design are clearly visible. The splendour of a horse's accoutrements were a direct reflection of the status of its owner. Many wealthy men had their horses killed and buried with them and, as a result, horse skeletons have been found in many Celtic burial sites, still decorated with intricately wrought harnesses and bits.

Fretted bronze plaque with enamelled decoration, probably belonging to a horse's harness.
The plaque dates from 1st–2nd centuries BC.

Battle Armour

Warriors rose together, formed ranks.
With a single mind they assaulted.
Short their lives, long their kinsmen long for them.
Seven times their sum of English they slew;
Their fighting turned wives into widows;
Many a mother with tear-filled lids.
Unknown Celtic Author, 'Y Gododdin'

The Celtic Hallstatt culture is noted for its metalwork, mostly in bronze, although iron was used in later pieces. The craftsmen used classical and oriental motifs, including palmetto and floral geometric designs. Sheet metalwork was often decorated with a series of punched dots forming a pattern. The work of the Hallstatt Celts was strong and vigorous, and although the ornamentation of their arms was somewhat rudimentary, it was none the less superior in many ways to that of their contemporaries. Arms and armour were essential to the Celts' tribal culture. They were a civilization of mounted raiders brandishing iron weapons, who spread rapidly over Europe from their home in south-west Germany, reaching the British Isles, France, Spain, Italy, Macedonia and Asia Minor. Their richly ornamental art was their most important cultural legacy, and their armour remains an emblem of their race.

Bronze-sheeted battle armour, decorated with a pattern of punched dots.
It dates from c. 8th century BC.

Amfreville Helmet

I see a battle: a blond man
with much blood about his belt
and a hero-halo round his head.
His brow is full of victories.
Unknown Celtic Author, 'The Tain'

mfreville-sous-les-Monts, in Eure, France, was the site of a spectacular archeological dig which uncovered what is now known as the Amfreville Helmet – a bronze helmet decorated with gold, enamel and iron bands, dating from the fourth century AD. The panels are open-work, filled with enamel, and the central gold leaf band has a series of linked figures consisting of three curved lines, or branches, radiating from a common centre. The helmet is flanked by two rows of hook-shaped and hatched waves – common details on pottery, metalwork and gravestones in fourth-century Greek and Etruscan art. This piece is thought to be an example of a style described as 'Waldalgesheim', or 'Vegetal'.

The Amfreville helmet dates from the late 4th century BC. It is decorated with gold repoussé
foliage-patterned sheets and inlaid with iron and enamel.

Bronze Shield

I do not know who it is
That fair Etain will go to bed with,
But I know that it is true
The fair Etain won't sleep alone.
Unknown Celtic Author, 'The Love of Etain'

This piece has become known as the 'Battersea Shield', as it was discovered in Battersea, South London. It is made of bronze and would have been used as a cover for a shield made of leather or wood. It has been impossible to date this piece precisely, but many experts believe that the symmetry of the cover, and the form of the outer roundels – as well as the use of glass inlay – point to the Roman occupation of Britain. The glass and enamel inlay is extraordinarily detailed and the high relief *repoussé* work of the three roundels, is unparalleled. Red glass decorates the inlays, and it is believed that this glass, like much of the glass used for Celtic inlay work, was of Mediterranean origin. Like many other examples of Celtic metalwork from the Iron Age, the Battersea Shield was found in England's River Thames – probably placed in the water to thank or appease the gods. In *The Celts*, Frank Delaney writes: 'The central box of the shield rises above the surrounding surface, roundel-decorated, too, a gleaming centrepiece, and so lavish and delicate seems the whole work, with inlaid glass and vivid colour, and abstract suggestions of fearsome facial expressions, that much speculation has focused on whether it was designed for battle at all … The lightness of the handle pinnings further raised the question as to whether the shield had ever been intended for combat, whether it possessed ceremonial or decorative status only.'

This shield was discovered at Battersea, London. Made of bronze with glass inlay,
it most probably dates from the Roman occupation of England.

Waterloo Helmet

Delightful land of honey and wine
Beyond what seems to thee most fair –
Rich fruits abound the bright year round
And flowers are found of hues most rare.

Unfailing there the honey and wine
And draughts divine of mead there be,
No ache nor ailing night or day –
Death or decay thou ne'er shalt see!

A hundred swords of steel refined,
A hundred cloaks of kind full rare,
A hundred steeds of proudest breed,
A hundred hounds – thy meed when there!

Unknown Celtic Author, 'The Land of Youth'

The Waterloo Helmet, as it has become known, was found in the River Thames, near London's Waterloo Bridge, in around 1866. It seems likely that the helmet dates from the first century BC. With its short conical horns this helmet is unique, and was once regarded as a jester's cap. It is made from two pieces of sheet bronze riveted together, with a third piece secured to the front, and decorated with an asymmetrical design including exquisite relief work and small *repoussé* lobes. Originally, the helmet was enamelled and may have been made to decorate a wooden statue, rather than to protect a warrior in battle.

This is one of the best-known prehistoric British objects, and one of the few Celtic helmets to have survived. Horned helmets are mentioned throughout early Irish literature; Furbaide Ferbend, for example, was said to have a three-horned helmet, two horns being of silver and one of gold.

Overleaf: The Waterloo Helmet was discovered under the Waterloo Bridge, London, in 1866. This horned piece is made of bronze inlayed with enamel – a characteristic Roman decoration.

Romano-Celtic Pyxis

The Father, the Son and the Holy Spirit,
May the Three in One be with us day and night.
Whether in the depths of the sea or on the mountainside,
May our Mother be with us, her arm around our heads.
Celtic blessing

A pyx, from the Greek word *puxis*, was used either as a container in which wafers for early Christian services were kept, or as a chest in a mint in which coins were placed to await assay. Before the Roman Conquest, decoration on metal trinkets and boxes was sparse; the Romans had an enormous influence on Celtic art, as well as providing a ready market for Celtic metalworkers, who developed a kind of 'tourist', or prettified, art in response to the demand. The enamel inlays on this small box were created using the *champlève* technique, in which powdered glass was inserted into a groove or space cut into the surface of the metal, and then heated to melt and fuse it. This type of enamelling was a trademark of the Celts; indeed, in the third century AD, the historian Philostratus wrote: 'They say that the barbarians who live in the Ocean pour colours on to heated bronze and that they adhere and grow hard as stone, keeping the designs that are made in them.'

Rare Romano-Celtic pyxis, made from bronze and inlaid with coloured enamel.
This piece dates from the 2nd–3rd centuries AD.

The Desborough Mirror

And the proud, cold girl like a ship in sail –
And what matter to you if their beauty founder,
If belly and breast will never be rounder,
If ready and glad to be mother and wife,
They drop unplucked from the boughs of life.
Unknown Celtic Author, 'The Midnight Court' (Cuirt an Mhean-Oiche)

The Desborough Mirror, dated to the first century AD, was discovered in Northamptonshire in 1908 and is now in the British Museum, in London. At this period in history, mirrors were widespread in the Roman world, but they were only rarely found among the Celts. The idea of polished metal mirrors was probably adopted from the classical world – in particular the Etruscans, the original inhabitants of the area around modern Rome, who were driven out by the Romans. Almost all Celtic burial sites where mirrors have been found are the graves of women. Most mirrors were cast in bronze, with the handle (usually composed of three parts) based on a looped lyre shape. The crescent rings and symmetrical designs were incised with a compass – a recurrent technique in Celtic art. The designs are infilled with a basketry pattern, or 'hatching', a feature which became characteristic of the 'Mirror Style' and is also found on scabbards and spears. According to a Celtic tradition, mirrors were kept upside down when not in use.

Bronze mirror discovered at Desborough in Northamptonshire. The back of this mirror is richly engraved with decorations, probably formed using a compass.

Second-Century Gold Coin

Colours of every shade glisten
throughout the gentle-voiced plains:
Joy is known, ranked around music,
In silver-cloud plain o the southward …
Unknown Celtic Author, 'The Isles of the Happy'

This gold Celtic coin is from north-west France and dates from the second century. Coins were first cast by metalsmiths as blank flans, and then laid between engraved metal dies and hammered. Their shape was always irregular, and a horse – occasionally riderless, frequently twin horses drawing a chariot – graced one or both sides of the coin. The horse motif appears to be more detailed in earlier coins, becoming more abstract and decorative in later styles. Interestingly, although they are important symbols of mythology, power and identity, horses are rarely portrayed in Celtic metalwork, except on coins. The idea of coins originated with the Greeks of Asia Minor and it was contact with Greek traders that introduced the idea to the Celts. They began minting their own copies of Greek coins in the late fourth century BC, and the designs of their coins clearly show a strong influence of the classical origins of coinage. As a result, the design of Celtic coins is less original than that of other Celtic art.

Gold coin dating from 2nd century AD. It shows two characteristics of Celtic coins –
an uneven outline and a decoration in the image of a horse.

The Gundestrup Cauldron

Summer dries the stream down small, the swift herd searches
for a pool. Heather spreads its hair afar. The pale bog-cotton,
faint, flourishes.
Ninth-century Celtic poem

Dating from the late second century BC, the Gundestrup Cauldron is a magnificent example of Celtic metalwork. It was found in a Danish peat bog in 1891, but is not Danish in origin. It was probably made in eastern Europe, although exactly where is not known. Most scholars believe that either eastern Hungary or Romania was the likely place of its origin, though a few believe that it could have been made as far east as Bulgaria.

The cauldron is made from plates of silver gilt, and more than one craftsman was involved in its making, for the style of the base-plate (not shown) is different to that of the sides. Before it was buried the cauldron was dismantled quite deliberately. Whatever the reason for this – probably to prevent it being stolen at a time of unrest and upheaval – not all the plates have survived. The symbolism of the figures and animals on what does remain of the cauldron is enigmatic. This is particularly tantalizing because the plates are well preserved and the figures extremely clear.

What purpose the cauldron served is unknown. Cauldrons certainly had a special place in early Celtic society and probably had some ritual purpose. Whatever its role, however, only a very rich chief or community could have commissioned a work like this.

The Gundestrup cauldron was discovered in a Danish peat bog. It is made of several silver-gilt
plates and dates from 2nd–1st century BC.

Bronze Enamelled Jewellery

The paintings are under glass,
or in dry rooms it is difficult
to breathe in; they are tired
of returning the hard stare of eyes...
R. S. Thomas

Red was a popular colour, frequently used by Celtic craftsmen for enamelling in this period, although green, yellow and blue were also used. Coral and red glass were usually imported from the Mediterranean for use in inlays. By the middle of the first century AD, when these pieces were created, most Celtic lands were under Roman rule. The Romans introduced the *millefiori* technique in which narrow rods of multi-coloured glass were fused together, sliced and then inlaid in red enamel. Bronze, and eventually silver, were finely crafted to display the intricate inlays. This selection of bronze jewellery represents both the *cloisonné* (where the enamel is inserted into cells formed by wire placed on the surface of the metal) and *champlève* (where the spaces are cut into the metal itself) techniques.

A selection of enamelled-bronze and bronze jewellery, including a rare Celtic bronze brooch of 'dragonesque' type, which dates from 50–150 AD.

Bronze Penannular Arm-ring

He is descended from a race of heroes,
a noble band, gold-helmed and generous.
Honoured, wealthy, hawk of men,
sturdy his limbs upon his horse;
swift to accomplish overthrow in battle,
a falcon excellently wise in argument,
a stag who does not die…
Dafydd (Celtic writer)

Traditional adornments for Celtic women seem to have been ring ornaments, particularly arm-rings and anklets. They also wore neck rings, although 'torques', as these were known, soon became the preserve of Celtic men. Any torque, brooch or arm-ring which does not form a complete ring is described as being 'penannular'. Such jewellery was popular in pre-Roman Britain as well as in the first and second centuries AD. By the fourth century they had become 'zoomorphic', a phrase coined by archeologists to describe a style of jewellery in which the ends of the brooch or arm-ring bear a resemblance to the head of an animal. This heavy arm-ring is cast in bronze and, compared to later examples, is relatively plain. As the rings became an established part of Celtic art, they became much more elaborate.

This very large bronze penannular armlet measures 9 cm in height and weighs 792 gm. It dates from 1st–2nd centuries AD.

Clonmacnois Torque

My chair is in Caer Siddi,
Where no one is affected with age or illness …
It is surrounded by three circles of fire.
To the borders of the city comes the ocean's flood
A fruitful fountain plays before it,
Whose liquor is sweeter than the finest wine.
Taliesin, 'The Defence of the Chair'

Where there is now nothing but peat bog, there was once a monastery in Clonmacnois, Co. Offaly, Ireland. Here, a virtual feast of Celtic treasures was uncovered – one of which was this gold piece called the Clonmacnois torque, dating from the 3rd century BC. The torque, of the 'Middle Rhine' type, is richly decorated with plant-based spirals. Torques were necklaces, which were worn mainly by Celtic men. This torque was probably imported to the monastery at Clonmacnois which is likely to have been both a centre for learning and a repository for objects of art and great beauty. The torque is an excellent example of the style of Celtic art known as La Tène art, which originated in what is now Switzerland. The La Tène period was characterized by highly creative metalworkers who manufactured a range of vessels and ornaments for their aristocratic patrons.

Torque discovered at the monastery in Clonmacnois, decorated with plant-based spirals. This piece dates from the 3rd century BC.

The Hunterston Brooch

First of summer, lovely sight,
season of perfection!
At the slightest ray the sun sends
blackbirds sing their full song.

The hardy vigorous cuckoo calls
all hail to high summer.
The bitter weather is abated
when the branched woods were torn …
Ninth-century Celtic poem

The Hunterston Brooch, which was found on a beach in Ayrshire, Scotland, is an excellent example of Celtic craftsmanship. The style has developed from the torque-like penannular brooches of an earlier date, but the terminals of this brooch are still clearly visible, so it is not yet a truly circular, or 'annular' brooch. The brooch is of solid silver, decorated with insets of gold, silver and amber, and was probably made by an Anglo-Saxon craftsman working for a Celtic patron, although many scholars believe the brooch to be Irish and suggest it was taken to Scotland by Norse invaders. It is dated to approximately AD 700, due to its similarity to the decorations within the Lindisfarne Gospels, including birds' heads, snouted beasts' heads and the

mathematical design. In the Dark Ages, the manufacture of penannular brooches flourished in Britain, created in the Romano-British workshops, with simple ornamentation that reflects the influence of the Romans and, later, the Anglo-Saxons on Celtic design.

The Hunterston Brooch is less extravagant than the Tara Brooch (see page 54), but it has a restrained, almost spiritual beauty. Brooches of this type were probably worn by bishops of the church, or by royalty. The Hunterston brooch is large – approximately 12.2 cm (4.8 in) across – and can be seen today on display in the Royal Museum at Edinburgh.

Above and Overleaf: The Hunterston Brooch is made of solid silver with gold, silver and amber insets. It probably belonged to a high-ranking church official or to royalty.

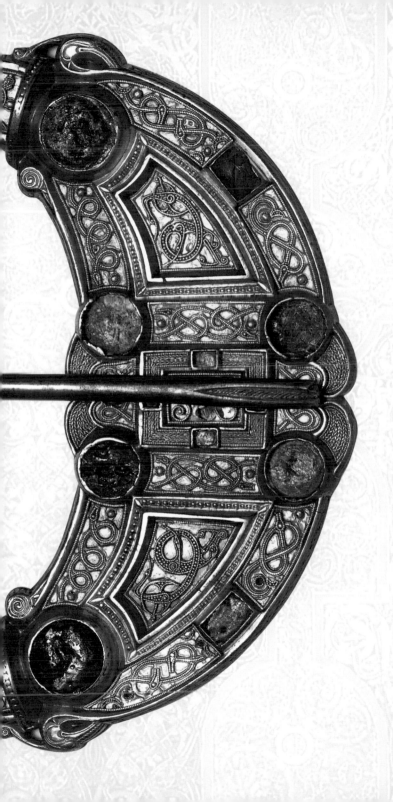

The Tara Brooch

Silent, O Moyle, be the roar of thy water;
Break not, ye breezes, your chain of repose,
While, murmuring mournfully, Lir's lonely daughter
Tells to the night-star her tale of woes.
When shall the swan, her death-note singing,
Sleep, with wings in darkness furl'd
When will my heaven, its sweet bells ringing,
Call my spirit from this stormy world?
Unknown Celtic Author, 'The Children of Lir'

The Tara Brooch, which is dated to the eighth century, was discovered in the nineteenth century in Bettystown, Co. Meath, Ireland. It was found in a wooden box near the banks of the River Boyne, along with several other objects of personal ornament. The brooch is an exquisite penannular of moulded bronze, decorated with panels of interwoven filigree birds and beasts, tiny human heads and inlays of red and blue glass. The miniature work is superb, covering both the front and back, and the brooch was probably one of a pair, worn on a tunic and joined across the shoulders with a silver chain. Animals with protruding eyes and curling lips fill the spaces and copper has been used in some of the larger panels. Its large size – almost 25 cm (10 in) in length and 8 cm (3 in) in diameter – designates it as a royal brooch. At the end of the Iron Age, brooches replaced torques as the insignia of royalty; the Tara Brooch was most likely associated with the kings of Meath.

The penannular brooch was introduced by the Romans, and the Irish school of delicate, bejewelled brooches is descended from this. Archeological evidence attests to the Celtic passion for personal decoration, and many brooches, finger-rings, arm-rings, anklets, necklets and elaborate metal belts have been found. The Greek historian and geographer, Strabo, wrote of the Celts around the first century AD, 'To the frankness and high-spiritedness of their temperament must be added the traits of childish boastfulness and love of decoration. They wear ornaments of gold, torques on their necks, and bracelets on their arms and wrists, while people of high rank wear dyed garments besprinkled with gold.'

Overleaf: The Tara Brooch is made of silver-gilt, intricately decorated with birds and animals and glass inlays in blue and red. It dates from the 8th century AD.

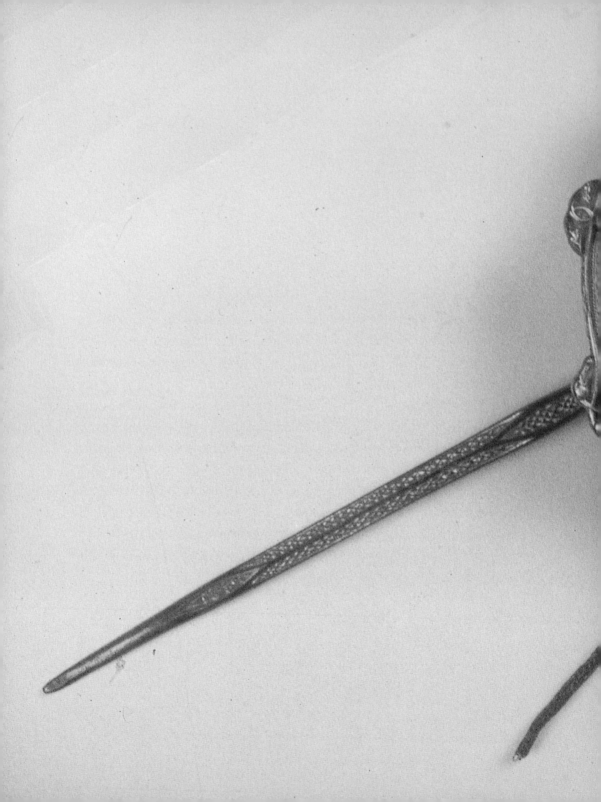

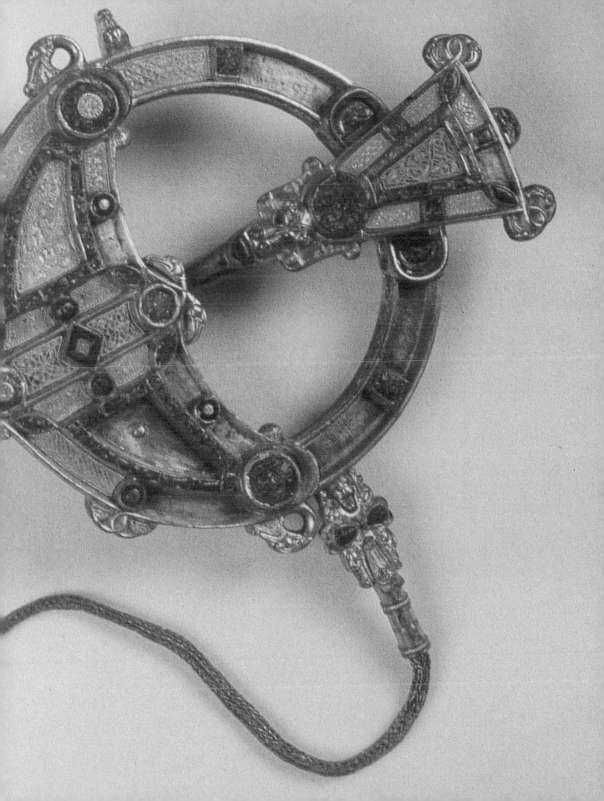

The Erstfeld Treasure

I arise today
Through the strength of heaven:
Light of sun,
Radiance of moon,
Splendour of fire,
Speed of lightning,
Swiftness of wind,
Depth of sea,
Stability of earth,
Firmness of Rock.
Blessing of the elements

The Erstfeld treasure, as this collection of finely wrought jewellery is known, was discovered in 1962 by a construction worker, who overturned a boulder and brought these extraordinary objects to light. They were discovered on the route to Italy in the southern Swiss valley of Erstfeld, and are too similar to other Rhineland pieces to be Italian. The jewellery is an excellent example of Celtic goldwork, dating from the late fifth or early fourth centuries BC, and is all thought to have been created by the same goldsmith. The jewellery is considered to be 'Insular Celtic', of the La Tène period. The imagery – plants and horned beasts are entwined with human figures,

birds and monsters – is characteristic of much Celtic workmanship of this date. Torques, the fine gold neck rings worn throughout the Celtic world, were not just items of jewellery, they were also units of wealth and status and symbols of divine power, with mystical and religious significance. Gold was the most popular metal and was used far more frequently than silver, although it was rarely used for brooches or bracelets. Unfortunately, due to their value, many gold items were melted down to make new jewellery and so are lost to us today. However, because gold does not corrode, the items which remain are as bright as on the day they were created.

This gold necklace from the Erstfeld Treasure shows intricate workings of human figures, animals, plants and monsters.

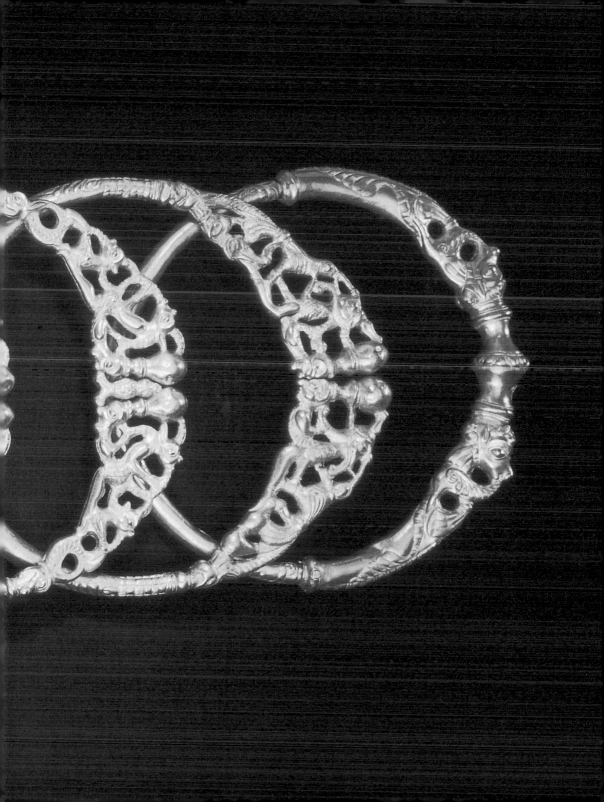

The Virgin and Child

In the hollow night of the senses, in the cauldron of smoke;
The great hair that had wiped his feet turned white,
All the flowers of memory withered except the rain of blood.
Saunders Lewis, 'Mary Magdalen'

The *Book of Kells*, which describes the life of Christ, is an extremely lavish and imaginative example of insular manuscript illumination, and it is believed that it was this book which Giraldus Cambrensis described, in about 1185, as 'the work of an angel, not a man'. Very little is known of its origin: it may be Irish or Scottish, and some experts believe it to be English. Its date is uncertain, probably sometime between the early eighth and early ninth centuries, and it has been suggested that it was made at Iona, Scotland, and that monks fled with it back to Ireland when Iona was sacked, in AD 806, by Vikings. The survivors of the Viking raids reached Kells (about thirty miles northwest of Dublin) where Cellach, the abbot of Iona, was buried in AD 815. Records show that the *Book of Kells* was at Kells by the twelfth century. This illumination of the Virgin and Child page exhibits the wealth of detail which characterizes the book as a whole.

The Virgin and Child is one of the most famous pages from the Book of Kells. *It has been dated to c. 8th century AD.*

Illumination of Christ

I was with my Lord in the highest sphere.
On the fall of Lucifer into the depths of Hell;
I know the names of the stars from north to south;
I have been on the galaxy at the throne of the Distributor;
I was in Canaan when Absalom was slain;
I conveyed the Divine Spirit to the level of the vale of Hebron.
Taliesin, 'The Mabinogion'

The story of the arrest of Christ was taken from the Gospel of St Matthew, and this illustration of it is one of the finest pages of the eighth-century *Book of Kells*. The intricacy of the decoration is unsurpassed: abstract forms, foliage patterns and beasts are intertwined into patterns of breathtaking complexity. The use of colour is sophisticated and uses pigments which must have been imported from Europe and the Far East. Many of the illustrations in the *Book of Kells* express insights attributed to St Columba and reflect aspects of Celtic culture. The garden of Gethsemane, above Christ's head on this page, is illustrated with symbols of the Pictish tree of life and Christ's divinity is represented by his blond hair. In battle, the Celts bleached their hair and thickened it with powdered lime to create a luminous effect.

Beautifully and intricately decorated page from the Book of Kells, *depicting Christ enthroned.*

Carpet Page from the *Lindisfarne Gospels*

I had my days with kings,
Drinking mead and wine:
Today I drink shey-water
Among the shrivelled old hags.
Dillon

Wonderful pages of multi-coloured abstract interlacing patterns, like this from the *Lindisfarne Gospels*, are characteristic of early Christian Celtic art. They are referred to as 'carpet pages'. Carpet pages appear on the left-hand page facing the beginning of each Gospel, and are there to mark each section and to help the priest to find his place quickly. Because the Gospel contained the revealed word of God, the beautiful illuminations on such pages are always painstakingly detailed. The rich ornamentation was a sign of honour and the elaborate illumination praised His word's mystery and complexity. Such work was intended to bring the essence of the word of God to an ill-educated audience; Bede described the effect of pictures in the church of Wearmouth 'to the intent that all ... even if ignorant of letters, might be able to contemplate ... the ever-gracious countenance of Christ and his saints ...'. St Gregory, the Pope who sent a Christian mission to England, said that a picture is a 'kind of literature for the uneducated man', and that is precisely what these brilliant illuminations were intended to be.

Highly ornamented carpet page from the Lindisfarne Gospels, *showing the vibrant colours and intricate patterns used throughout the book.*

The Evangelists' Symbols

In the beginning was the Word, and the Word was with God,
and the Word was God. The same was in the beginning with
God. All things were made by him; and without him was not
anything made that was made.

St John, I:1-3

The symbol for St John is the eagle, and he is depicted here as a highly stylized eagle surrounded by elaborate scrollwork, crosses and interlacing. It was believed that the Apostle's symbols on the opening pages of each one's Gospel were talismans to keep evil from the treasure in the book. Uncial, Latin for 'inch-high' letters, were a Roman adaptation of a contemporary Greek hand. In England and Ireland a special style of uncial and half uncial letters, named 'insular', developed in the seventh century. The best-known examples are in the *Lindisfarne Gospels* and the *Book of Kells*. The *Book of Kells* is the most famous, and the last, of the great Insular Gospel books. It is from these rounded, unjoined letters that our modern capital letters derive.

The Evangelists' symbols appeared on the opening pages of each Gospel and were believed to
be a deterrent to evil. This is the eagle of St John.

The Eagle of St John

I saw the Weaver of Dreams, an immortal
shape of star-eyed Silence; and the Weaver of Death, a lovely
Dusk with a heart of hidden flame; and each wove with the
shuttles of beauty and Wonder and mystery … Come unto me,
O Lovely Dusk, thou that has the heart of hidden flame.
Fiona MacLeod, *The Silence of Amor*

The Eagle symbol for St John the Evangelist in the *Book of Durrow* introduces the last of the four Gospels and is much simpler than its counterpart in the *Book of Kells*. The beautiful knotted fretwork surrounds a carefully restrained white background. The head of the eagle, like the other symbols in the book, is Germanic, and the torso shows a Pictish influence. The *Book of Durrow* has aroused some controversy due to the invocation at its conclusion which asks that whoever holds the book in his hands should remember Columba its scribe, who copied it in twelve days. This inscription, however, has been altered and rewritten, creating doubt about its authenticity. It is possible that the book comes from one of St Columba's foundations (of which Durrow, in Ireland, is one) some time in the second half of the seventh century. Experts argue about where the book was created: Ireland, Iona or at Lindisfarne – it is certainly small enough to have been carried in a traveller's pack.

The eagle of St John which appears in the Book of Durrow *(c. 8th century AD) is more simplistic than St John's eagle depicted in the* Book of Kells.

Carpet Page from the *Book of Durrow*

O heart of the valour of Western lands
My heart will go near to breaking
If I do not see you every day. The parting of the two of us
Will be the parting of two children
Of the one house;
It will be the parting of life from the body,
Diarmuid, hero of the bright lake of Carmen.
Unknown Celtic Author, 'Diarmuid and Grainne'

he *Book of Durrow* is not a large book – it measures only 20 x 15 cm (8 x 6 in) – but it is filled with wonderfully luxuriant embellishments, coloured with lemon yellow, warm red and deep green. It contains especially fine carpet pages: whole-page abstract, multi-coloured designs of amazing complexity at which the Irish excelled. The intricate patterns are intended to illustrate the interconnection of all things, and the eternity offered by Christ through the Gospels. The *Book of Durrow* has six elaborate carpet pages of interlaced patterns, of which this is one. When carpet pages include the Christian cross, they are called 'cross carpet' pages. The animal interlace echoes a Germanic influence, while the central roundel is distinctly Celtic.

Carpet page from the Book of Durrow, *showing the luxurious textured effects of the abstract, brightly-coloured designs.*

First Page of St Matthew's Gospel

On the ocean that hollows the rocks where ye dwell
A shadowy land has appeared as they tell;
Men thought it a region of sunshine and rest
And they called it Hy-Brasil, the Isle of the Blest.
Celtic narrative poem

The *Lindisfarne Gospels*, from which this illustration comes, dates from around AD 700, and was produced at the monastery at Lindisfarne on Holy Island, an inhospitable island off the Northumbrian coast of Britain. The book is believed to have taken about two years to complete and is the work of a single scribe, who also created the illuminations. It is a work of outstanding beauty and sophistication, and was possibly meant to be displayed with the body of St Cuthbert, a saint and hermit who was reburied in an elaborate shrine at Lindisfarne. The *Lindisfarne Gospels* is the most complete Gospel book to have survived from the seventh century, and contains marvellous miniatures of the Apostles – Matthew, Mark, Luke and John – each with his own symbol; the winged man is symbolic of Matthew.

First page from the Gospel of St Matthew in the Lindisfarne Gospels, *dating from c. AD 700.*

imagohominis: MACES HATHEUS

Illuminated Initial from St Matthew's Gospel

Lay not up for yourselves treasures upon earth, where moth and rust doth corrupt, and where thieves break through and steal: But lay up for yourselves treasures in heaven, where neither moth nor rust doth corrupt, and where thieves do not break through nor steal: For where your treasure is, there will your heart also be.

St Matthew, I: 19-21

The opening words of St Matthew's Gospel in the *Book of Kells* are decorated with magnificently illuminated initials. No other Christian manuscript in western Europe is as splendid as the *Book of Kells*: only two of its 680 pages have no colour. The colours are limited – mainly yellow, deep red, brown and green – but the technique is far more lavish than that seen in the earlier, smaller Gospel books. For the first time, initials are decorated with plaited, intricate interlacings which extend the contours of the letters in a dramatic and unique way. Cambrensis wrote of the *Book of Kells*: 'Here you can look upon the face of the divine majesty drawn in a miraculous way; here too upon the mystical representations of the Evangelists now having six, now four, and now two wings. Here you will see the eagle; there the calf. Here the face of a man; there that of a lion … '.

The opening words of St Matthew's Gospel in the Book of Kells *are decorated with intricate illuminated initials.*

Illustrated Page from St Matthew's Gospel

I am the God who creates in the head the fire
Who is it who throws light into the meeting on the mountain?
Who announces the ages of the moon?
Who teaches the place where the sun lies?
Who callest the cattle from the House of Tethra
On whom do the cattle of Tethra smile?
Who is the God who fashions edges?
Changements about a spear?
Enchantments of wind?

Dillon

Another magnificent illumination in the *Lindisfarne Gospels* is this, which appears in Chapter I, Verse 18, at the beginning of St Matthew's account of the incarnation of Christ. The huge Greek letters, XPI, form the monogram for the sacred name of Christ. The most highly decorated pages of the Gospels were composed of pure ornament, amazingly intricate with many varieties of plaits and knotwork, keys, fretwork, and spiral patterns, contorted and interlaced birds and animals. Smaller, less important initials, such as those of St Matthew's, which appear here, were highlighted with dabs of colour, often green or yellow, and outlined with the pink dots characteristic of this style.

Illustrated page from the Gospel of St Matthew in the Lindisfarne Gospels, *showing the Greek letters XPI. These letters indicate the sacred name of Christ.*

Initial Page of St Mark's Gospel

---

*From the earliest times the Celts displayed a love of ornamentation and their art is
dominated by spiral patterns, curvilinear designs, foliage motifs, plant tendrils scrolls,
trumpet scrolls, zig-zags, loops, simple geometric shapes, palmettes and triskeles.*

O. B. Duane, *Celtic Art*

The *Book of Durrow,* which contains the gospels of the four Apostles, Matthew, Mark, Luke and John, was written in the second half of the seventh century. No one knows who wrote it, or even where it was written. Most scholars believe it was written in Ireland, although some argue it may, perhaps, have been written in Northumbria, as there were strong links between the Christian communities in these two places at that time.

The unknown scribe worked on fine vellum, as befitted the importance of the book. The colours he used were largely limited to yellow, vermilion, green and brownish-black. This may have been a deliberate choice, with the intention of increasing the impact by using less colours (in the same way that some photographs are more effective in black and white). Alternatively, it may merely reflect the colours that were available at the time. We do not know. Certainly, the *Book of Kells*, written less than 100 years later, uses a much wider range of colours. Whatever the reason, however, the complexity and sophistication of the patterns more than compensate for the lack of colour.

In the *Book of Durrow*, for the first time, the spirals, plaiting and complex interwoven designs that are so characteristic of Celtic art cease to be purely abstract. They evolve into the creatures that are the Apostle's symbols, so setting a style that later scribes would follow.

This initial page from the Gospel of St Mark in the Book of Durrow *exhibits more limited
ornamentation than the* Book of Kells *or the* Lindisfarne Gospels.

incipit euangelium
secundum marcum

INITIUM
EUANGE
LII IHU XPI
filii di sicut sc
riptum in esaia
profeta. ecce mitto an
gelum meum ante faciem
tuam qui praeparabit uiam tuam
UOX clamantis in deser
to parate uiam dni rec
tas facite semitas eius
FUIT iohannis in deserto
babtizans et praedicans
babtismum paenitentiae

St Patrick's Bell Shrine

Mothers of our mother,
Foremothers strong.
Guide our hands in yours,
Remind us how to kindle the hearth,
To keep it bright,
To preserve the flame.
Your hands upon ours,
Our hands within yours,
To kindle the light,
Both day and night.
Celtic blessing

St Patrick's Bell Shrine is likely to have been made in Armagh, between AD 1091 and 1105. It is thought to have been produced by Irish craftsmen, although influenced by Scandinavian design. It was created by order of the King of Ireland and used as a shrine for a bell which was a relic of St Patrick, the patron saint of Ireland, and the man who brought Christianity to the country. Patrick was a monk whose success lay in his ability to incorporate Christian beliefs into existing druidic and religious patterns. He is also believed to have purged Ireland of snakes. The shrine is made of bronze and decorated with elaborate filigree – wire which is polished and twisted and then soldered to the bronze shrine. Despite the evidence of Scandinavian influences in the design, the greatest influence on Celtic society and art was that of the Christian faith, and shrines like this illustrate the enthusiasm and devotion of the Celtic craftsman.

St Patrick's Bell Shrine was probably made by Irish craftsmen despite the obvious
Scandinavian influences. It is fashioned from bronze and filigree.

The Lismore Crosier

The desire of the fairy women: dew.
The desire of the fairy host: wind.
The desire of the raven: blood.
The desire of the snipe: the wilderness.
The desire of the seamen: the lawns of the sea.
The desire of the poet: the soft low music
of the Tribe of the Green Mantles.
The desire of man: the love of woman.
The desire of women: the little clan.
The desire of the soul: wisdom.
Fiona MacLeod, 'The Hills of Dream'

The Lismore Crosier, which was presented to the Bishop of Lismore, in Co. Waterford, in the early twelfth century, is one of the most intricate to have been produced in Ireland. The crosier is bronze, shaped like a seahorse, and dates from roughly the same period as the St Patrick's Bell Shrine (*c.* AD 1100). Archeologists believe that the crook of the crosier probably held good filigree work; the shaft is studded with glass millefiori, with cross designs and the remains of what was once heavy gilding. Beasts and human heads embellish the design. The decorative knobs are a special feature, adorned as they are with gold filigree, coloured glass studs and exquisite engraving.

The Lismore Crosier dates from c. AD 1100. It is embellished with gold filigree, glass studs in red, blue and white, and delicate engravings.

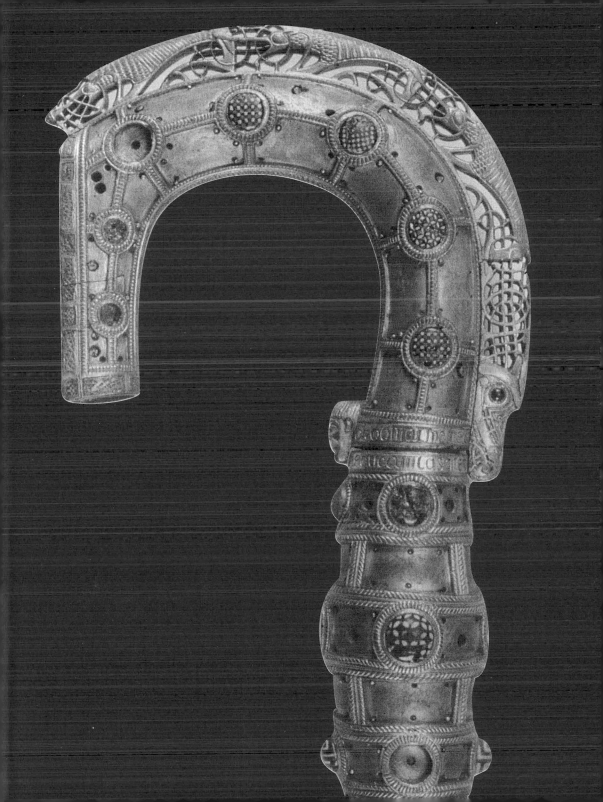

The Cross of Cong

Buds break out on the hawthorn bush.
The sea runs its calm course
– the salt sea the season soothes.
Blossom blankets the world.
Ninth-century Celtic poem

This beautiful piece of Irish metalwork is one of the most perfect examples of late Celtic art. Known to have been created at the request of Turlough O'Connor, the King of Connacht, it has been dated to AD 1123. At the centre of the highly ornate cross, is a rock crystal, this protects a supposed fragment of the True Cross – the cross on which Christ was crucified – one of the most revered relics in the Christian world.

The body of the Cross of Cong was made of wood, this was then covered in filigree-worked copper and sheets of silver, and the metals were then riveted together. At carefully spaced points along the front of this casing were inserted small pieces of glass and enamel. The back of the cross is decorated with four panels of Urnes-style animals: the Urnes style, introduced in AD 1050, was named after a wooden church in Norway; it is typified by patterns created from elongated tendrils of foliage carved on metalwork. The animal ornament, shown here at the base of the cross, is considered to be one of the finest examples of Urnes-style Irish art ever found.

Unfortunately not visible in this picture, the silver sides of the Cross of Cong are engraved with various inscriptions. One of these inscriptions gives the name of Maelisu as the artist who created this unique piece.

The Cross of Cong was created in AD 1123 for the King of Connacht. It is made from oak encased in copper and silver sheets with beautiful and intricate engraving.

St John's Crucifixion Plaque

*Metalwork was a specialized skill of the Celtic craftsmen and
the roots of Celtic art are best traced in metal objects. The
artists used combinations of iron, bronze, gold and also silver
in the many objects they produced, both secular and religious.*
O. B. Duane, *Celtic Art*

Metalworking flourished in Ireland from the sixth century, but if the evidence of what
has survived is correct, it was principally confined to secular objects. The earliest
surviving piece of religious metalwork is probably the St John's Crucifixion Plaque
from Athlone in the south of Ireland, which dates from the late seventh century.

The piece, which is made of gilt-bronze, shows Christ nailed to the cross. Above
him are two angels, one of which is holding something that could be a stylized musical
instrument. Below are two other figures: one carrying a spear and the other a sponge.
These figures are probably an allusion to the accounts of the Crucifixion in the gospels
of Matthew, Mark and John in which soldiers offered Christ a sponge soaked in vinegar
while in agony on the cross.

The patterns with which the figures on the plaque are decorated are typical of
Celtic art. They appear in metalwork, carving, jewellery and, of course, works like the
Book of Durrow, which was probably a contemporary of this piece. The purpose of the
plaque is unclear: it could have been used as the cover of a book, such as a copy of
the Bible, or to decorate a shrine containing the relics of a saint.

*St John's Crucifixion Plaque is made of gilt-bronze. It is possibly the earliest Celtic work
depicting the crucifixion and dates from the late 7th century AD.*

Illustration Notes

Page 10 *The Cross of Cong* (National Museum of Ireland, Dublin). Courtesy of Visual Arts Library. **Page 13** *Celtic Rain Chariot in the Form of a Bird*. Courtesy of Christie's Images. **Page 15** *Selection of Small Bronze Figures of Animals*. Courtesy of Christie's Images. **Page 17** *Romano-Celtic Bronze Statuette of a Standing Deity and Roman Bronze Figure of Athena*. Courtesy of Christie's Images. **Page 19** *Dieu de Bouray* (Musée des Antiquités Nationàles, St Germain). Courtesy of Visual Arts Library. **Page 21** *Stone Figure, Armagh, St Patrick's Cathedral*. Courtesy of Visual Arts Library. **Page 23** *Carved Wooden Figure from Ralaghan*. Courtesy of the National Museum of Ireland, Dublin. **Page 25** *Fretted Bronze Plaque with Enamelled Decoration* (Musée Archaeologique de Breteuil). Courtesy of Werner Forman Archive. **Page 27** *Bronze Sheeted Battle Armour* (Musée des Antiquités Nationales, St Germain). Courtesy of Visual Arts Library. **Page 29** *Am]reville Helmet* (Réunion des Musées Nationaux, Paris). Courtesy of Visual Arts Library. **Page 31** *Bronze Shield Discovered at Battersea* (British Museum, London). Courtesy of Visual Arts Library. **Pages 34-5** *Bronze Horned Helmet and Enamel Inlay* (British Museum, London). Courtesy of Visual Arts Library. **Page 37** *Rare Romano-Celtic Inlaid Bronze Pyxis*. Courtesy of Christie's Images. **Page 39** *Bronze Mirror with Richly Engraved Back* (British Museum, London). Courtesy of Werner Forman Archive. **Page 41** *Gold Slater of the Aucerll Cenomani* (British Museum, London). Courtesy of Visual Arts Library. **Page 43** *Gundestrup Cauldron* (National Museum, Copenhagen). Courtesy of Visual Arts Library. **Pages 44-5** *Selection of Enamelled Bronze and Bronze Jewellery*. Courtesy of Christie's Images. **Page 47** *Celtic Massive Bronze Penannular Armlet*. Courtesy of Christie's Images. **Page 49** *Clonmacnois Gold Torque* (National Museum of Ireland, Dublin). Courtesy of Visual Arts Library. **Page 51** Detail from *Hunterston Brooch* (Royal Museum of Scotland, Edinburgh). Courtesy of Visual Arts Library. **Pages 52-3** *Hunterston Brooch* (Royal Museum of Scotland, Edinburgh). Courtesy of Visual Arts Library. **Pages 56-7** *Tara Brooch* (National Museum of Ireland, Dublin). Courtesy of Visual Arts Library. **Page 59** Detail from *Gold Necklace from the Erstfeld Treasure* (Musée Nationale Suisse, Zurich). Courtesy of Visual Arts Library. **Pages 60-1** *Gold Necklace from the Erstfeld Treasure* (Musée Nationale Suisse, Zurich). Courtesy of Visual Arts Library. **Page 63** *Virgin and Child from the Book of Kells* (Trinity College, Dublin). Courtesy of Visual Arts Library. **Page 65** *Christ from the Book of Kells* (Trinity College, Dublin). Courtesy of Visual Arts Library. **Page 67** *Carpet Page from the Lindisfarne Gospels*. Courtesy of Visual Arts Library. **Page 69** *Evangelists from the Book of Kells* (Trinity College, Dublin). Courtesy of Visual Arts Library. **Page 71** *Eagle Emblem of St John from the Book of Durrow* (Trinity College, Dublin). Courtesy of Visual Arts Library. **Page 73** *Carpet Page from the Book of Durrow* (Trinity College, Dublin). Courtesy of Visual Arts Library. **Page 75** *St Matthew from the Lindisfarne Gospels* (British Library, London). Courtesy of Visual Arts Library. **Page 77** *Opening Words St Matthew's Gospel from the Book of Kells* (Trinity College, Dublin). Courtesy of Visual Arts Library. **Page 79** *Incarnation Initial from the Lindisfarne Gospels* (British Library, London). Courtesy of Visual Arts Library. **Page 81** *Initial Page of St Mark's Gospel from the Book of Durrow* (Trinity College, Dublin). Courtesy of Visual Arts Library. **Page 83** *St Patrick's Bell Shrine* (National Museum of Ireland, Dublin). Courtesy of Visual Arts Library. **Page 85** *Lismore Crosier* (National Museum of Ireland, Dublin). Courtesy of Visual Arts Library. **Page 87** *Cross of Cong* (National Museum of Ireland, Dublin). Courtesy of Visual Arts Library. **Page 89** *St John's Crucifixion Plaque* (National Museum of Ireland, Dublin). Courtesy of Visual Arts Library.

Index